For James x
- SGC

DK | Penguin Random House

Author Sital Gorasia Chapman
Illustrator Susanna Rumiz

Editor Laura Gilbert
Senior Designer Elle Ward
US Senior Editor Shannon Beatty
Math Consultant Steph King
Production Editor Abi Maxwell
Production Controller Magdalena Bojko
Jacket Coordinator Magda Pszuk
Deputy Art Director Mabel Chan
Publisher Francesca Young
Publishing Director Sarah Larter

First American Edition, 2023
Published in the United States by DK Publishing
1745 Broadway, 20th Floor, New York, NY 10019

23 24 25 26 27 10 9 8 7 6 5 4 3 2 1
001–332640–May/2023
Published in Great Britain by Dorling Kindersley Limited
A catalog record for this book is available from the
Library of Congress.

ISBN: 978-0-7440-8024-7

DK books are available at special discounts when purchased
in bulk for sales promotions, premiums, fund-raising, or
educational use. For details, contact: DK Publishing Special
Markets, 1745 Broadway, 20th Floor, New York, NY 10019
SpecialSales@dk.com

Printed and bound in China

For the curious
www.dk.com

MIX
Paper | Supporting
responsible forestry
FSC™ C018179

This book was made with Forest
Stewardship Council™ certified
paper - one small step in DK's
commitment to a sustainable future.
**For more information go to
www.dk.com/our-green-pledge**

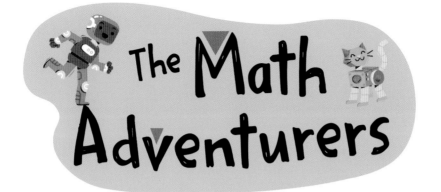

The Math Adventurers

Build a Friendship

Beep gazed out the window
and watched the children play
with their puppies and their kittens.
They had fun and games all day.

She wished that she could have a pet
to call her very own,
a loyal friend to play with
so she'd never feel alone.

Beep wished on all the stars that night
until she closed her eyes.
And when she woke up from her sleep,
she had a big surprise.

An early morning delivery
had been left at Beep's door.
"To Beep," it said, "with lots of love,
you'll be alone no more."

"What could it be?" she wondered,
and eager to find out,
she ripped the wrapping off
and let out a happy shout.

Beep's wishes had been answered
by a secret mathematician.
She'd build herself a little friend—
a cute robotic kitten.

Turning the box upside down,
she shook the contents on the ground.

Parts, all shapes and all dimensions,
scattered all around.

Octagons with eight straight sides
and rectangles with four,
circles with no corners,
all tumbled to the floor.

2-D shapes, like squares and rectangles, are flat and have two dimensions— **length** and **width**.

length ↕ width ↔

There were pentagons and hexagons,
a triangle-shaped nose,
curvy shapes and pointy shapes.
She laid them out in rows.

Beep fit the parts together
and made herself a cat.
But something didn't seem quite right,
it looked a little flat.

You can't actually pick up and hold a **2-D** shape. Next time the sun is out, look at your shadow on the ground and try to pick it up! That is a **2-D** shape.

As she pulled it to its feet,
the pieces fell apart.
They tumbled to the floor again.
She was right back at the start.

Then from the corner of her eye
Beep spotted something tiny.
Hidden deep inside the box,
a wand, star-shaped and shiny.

circle

sphere

square

She pointed at a circle
and it popped into a sphere.

triangle

cube

cone

A square became a cube,
a triangle, a cone-shaped ear.

A **square** is a type of **rectangle**, where all four straight sides are the same length and all four corners are **right angles**.

← right angle

Rectangles curled into cylinders,
three for each cat limb.
Eight small bits to make a tail,
curved, long, and slim.

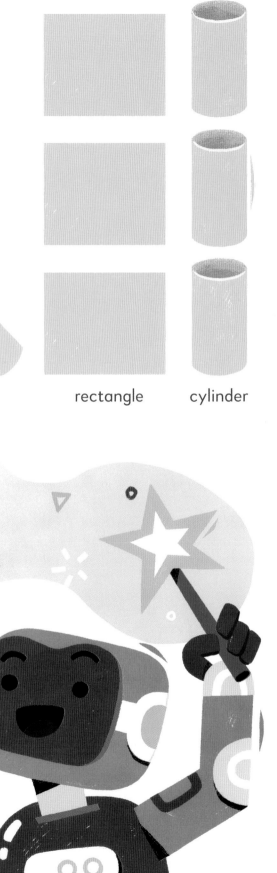

rectangle   cylinder

All the parts that once were flat,
made three-dimensional.
Beep could build her robot now.
It was just phenomenal!

She stacked up cones and cylinders,
a really big cuboid,
prisms, spheres, and pyramids,
to build her cat android.

3-D shapes, like cubes and pyramids, are solid and have three dimensions—**length**, **width**, and **height**. The page you're reading now might seem flat but you can hold it, so it is **3-D**!

But the robot didn't look much like
the picture on the box.
Beep tried and tried and tried again
to rearrange the blocks.

Different patterns and positions,
she tried and tried them all.
But nothing seemed to work quite right.
And she watched the pieces fall.

Beep was so frustrated.
She didn't have her pet.
She'd have to start all over,
but she couldn't give up yet.

She followed the instructions,
numbers 1 to 24,
and step by step she built it up
from tail to final paw.

The robot looked just perfect,
but it didn't move a bit.
It didn't make a single sound.
"Now, what's wrong with it?"

Something was still missing.
Beep sat down to think.
And something caught her eye again—
something glowing, something pink.

Beep had missed the final step,
the most important part.
Carefully she put it in...

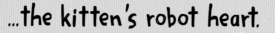

...the kitten's robot heart.

With whizzes, whirrs, and flashes,
meeps and beeps, a click,
Boots opened up her eyes
and gave her tail a flick.

This was the beginning
of adventures with no end
for Boots, the robot kitten,
and Beep, her new best friend.

GLOSSARY

2-D Shapes

2-D or two-dimensional shapes are flat and can't be picked up. They have a length and width.

Circle—a round shape where the center is equal distance from every point of its curved side

Octagon—a shape with 8 straight sides and 8 corners (or vertices)

Hexagon—a shape with 6 straight sides and 6 corners (or vertices)

Pentagon—a shape with 5 straight sides and 5 corners (or vertices)

Square—a 4-sided shape where all sides are the same length and all corners are right angles

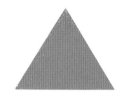

Triangle—a shape with 3 straight sides and 3 corners (or vertices)

Semicircle—half a circle

Rectangle—a 4-sided shape where the opposite sides are the same length and all corners are right angles

3-D Shapes

3-D or three-dimensional shapes are solid and can be picked up. They have a length, width, and height.

Cone—a shape with a flat circular base and a curved surface that narrows to a point

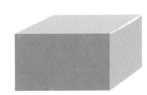

Cuboid—a shape with 6 rectangular faces, 8 vertices, and 12 edges

Sphere—a round shape where the centre is the same distance from every point on its surface

Cube—a shape with 6 square faces, 8 vertices, and 12 edges

Prism—a shape with 2 identical straight-edged faces joined by rectangular faces

Cylinder—a shape with 2 identical flat circular faces joined by a curved surface

Square-based pyramid—a shape with a square base and four triangular faces that meet at a vertex

Describing shapes

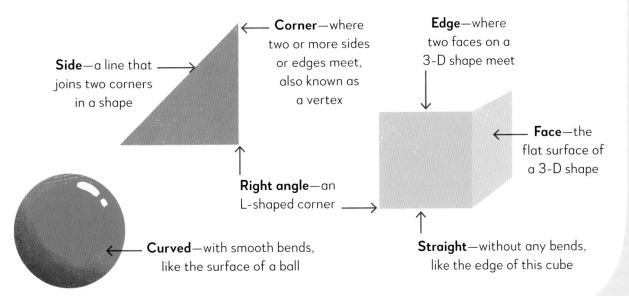

Side—a line that joins two corners in a shape

Corner—where two or more sides or edges meet, also known as a vertex

Edge—where two faces on a 3-D shape meet

Face—the flat surface of a 3-D shape

Right angle—an L-shaped corner

Curved—with smooth bends, like the surface of a ball

Straight—without any bends, like the edge of this cube

QUESTIONS

1. What do we call a 2-D shape with 3 straight sides?

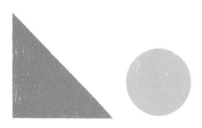

2. Are these shapes all rectangles?

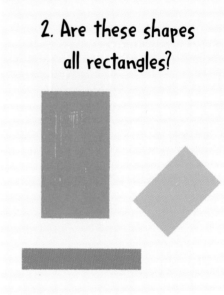

3. Which 2-D shape has no corners (vertices)?

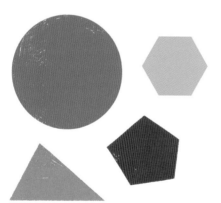

4. How many corners does an octagon have?

5. Is a pyramid a 2-D shape or a 3-D shape?

6. This cube has 6 faces. What shape are they all?

7. Look in your kitchen or in a store. What shape is a can of food?

8. What shape are your windows?

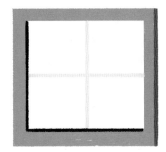

9. Can you find any cuboids around you?

10. Which shapes roll best?

Answers: see page 32

ANSWERS

1. A triangle
2. Yes
3. A circle
4. 8

5. A pyramid is a 3-D shape
6. They are all squares
7. A cylinder
10. A sphere or cylinder